Country Vet

Have you ever wondered what happens
when an animal goes to the doctor?
Take a visit to the country vet and
find out.

by Bernadette Kelly

800-445-5985
www.etacuisenaire.com

Country Vet
ISBN 0-7406-4143-3
ETA 383041

ETA/Cuisenaire • Vernon Hills, IL 60061-1862
800-445-5985 • www.etacuisenaire.com

ETA/Cuisenaire
Manager of Product Development: Mary Watanabe
Creative Services Manager: Barry Daniel Petersen
Production Manager: Jeanette Pletsch
Lead Editor: Betty Hey
Copy Editor: Barbara Wrobel
Production Artist: Diana Chiropolos
Graphic Designer: Amy Endlich

Photographs on pp. iv, 1–12, 23–27, and cover by Natalie Stitt
Photographs on pp. 19–22 by Bernadette Kelly

Teacher consultant: Garry Chapman, Ivanhoe Grammar School

Printed in China.

06 07 08 09 10 11 12 13 14 15   10 9 8 7 6 5 4 3 2 1

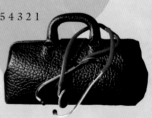

Contents

Andrew   **Kellie**

Peter

Chapter One

Sick Pony

My son Tom has a sick pony. Flika has a runny nose and a cough. Tom is worried.

We think we should take Flika to see the vet. I call the **animal clinic** to let them know we are coming.

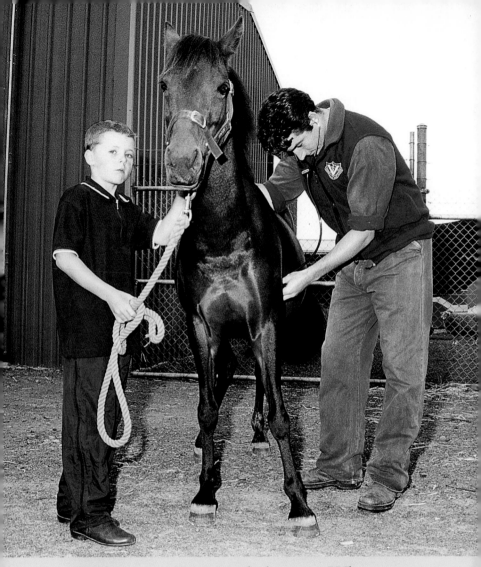

Andrew is an animal doctor. When we arrive at the clinic, he comes outside to examine Flika.

He checks her temperature and listens to her breathing. Andrew asks Tom some questions about Flika's cough.

Andrew says that Flika has a cold. Andrew thinks she will be fine after a few days' rest. Tom is pleased to hear that Flika can go home and that she will not need any medicine to help her get better.

Tom stays with Flika while I go inside
the clinic to settle the account. This looks
like an interesting place. I ask Jana, the vet
technician, what happens at a veterinary clinic.

Jana says, "If you come back tomorrow,
you can see for yourself."

Chapter Two

Vets at Work

The next morning, I arrive at the animal clinic to find Jana checking the medicines. It's important to have plenty of supplies.

There are four vets here: Peter, David, Kellie, and Andrew. The vet technicians are Jana, Linda, and Amanda. This is a busy clinic.

Linda takes me to see the hospital ward. This is where sick animals are kept overnight, or sometimes longer.

Sometimes the animals must stay to recover from an operation. Buddy, a dog, is not very happy to be here.

Every morning, Amanda gives the animals
breakfast and fresh water. She also puts fresh
newspaper on the bottom of each cage.

The cats stay in their cages, but Amanda
takes each dog out for a walk. Jake is
pleased to be out of his cage.

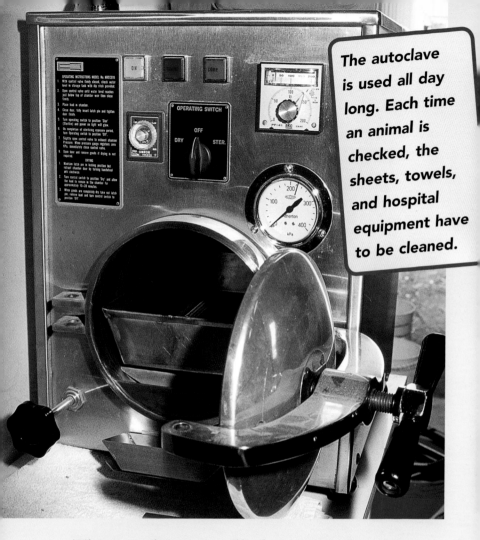

The autoclave is used all day long. Each time an animal is checked, the sheets, towels, and hospital equipment have to be cleaned.

This machine is called an autoclave. It is a steam **sterilizing** [STARE-a-lie-zing] machine that is used to remove any germs that may be on the surgical equipment. Sheets and towels are sterilized as well.

The animal clinic must be kept very clean, just like a hospital for people.

In the waiting room, people are already arriving with their pets. Linda asks their names and the names of their animals.

Andrew calls the next pet, Charlie, and his owner into the consulting room.

Like doctors, vets do a check-up on each patient and keep a record of each patient's health.

Charlie is a bulldog. He's having a check-up. Andrew listens to Charlie's heart with a **stethoscope** [STETH-a-scope]. He takes Charlie's temperature and looks in his eyes and ears. Charlie is fine. He can go home.

Butch has been acting strangely. He has no energy, and he doesn't want his food. His owner hopes that the vet can help him.

Butch sniffs the floor. There are lots of animal smells in here.

Each animal has its details recorded on a chart on its cage. The chart has its name, the name of its owner, and its medical history.

Andrew cannot tell right away what is wrong with Butch. Butch will have to stay in the hospital ward for observation.

Amanda puts Butch into a cage. Every few hours, one of the vets will take Butch out and examine him.

Chapter Three

Smithy's Operation

A harness race is a type of horse race. Each horse has a driver who rides in a two-wheeled cart called a sulky.

Smithy is a harness racehorse, but he has a problem. He makes a loud roaring noise when he runs very fast. That's because he can't get enough air in his **windpipe**.

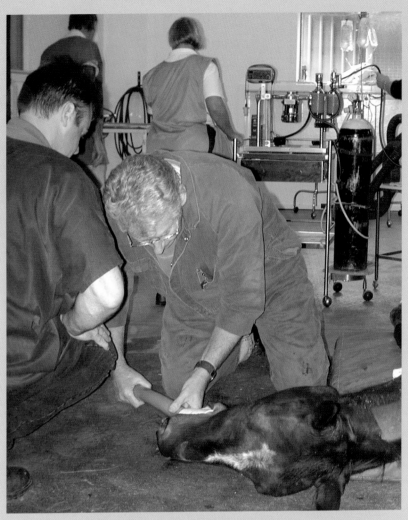

Vic is a horse **specialist**. He will operate on Smithy to help him get more air and stop the roaring noise.

Peter, David, and the technicians will all help.

Smithy lies on a mattress which is on a movable metal slab. It is so heavy, it can only be moved using a forklift.

Smithy is given an injection to help him relax. The technicians make sure he is comfortable. His feet are bandaged so that he cannot injure himself during the operation.

Shaving the hair around Smithy's neck makes it easier to operate. Smithy's injury will heal before the hair grows back.

Smithy's neck is shaved so that it can be thoroughly cleaned before Vic does the operation. Keeping the area clean helps to prevent **infection**.

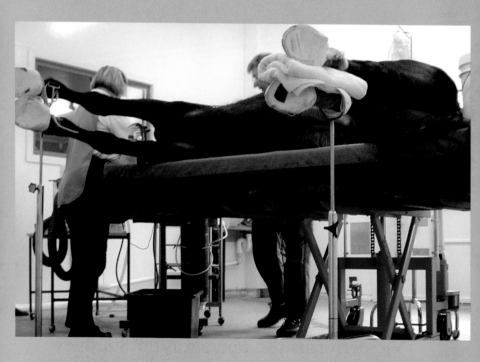

After the operation, Smithy will find it much easier to breathe when he is racing.

Smithy is given an injection to help him sleep. He will need a machine to help him breathe while he is asleep, so a tube is put into his mouth.

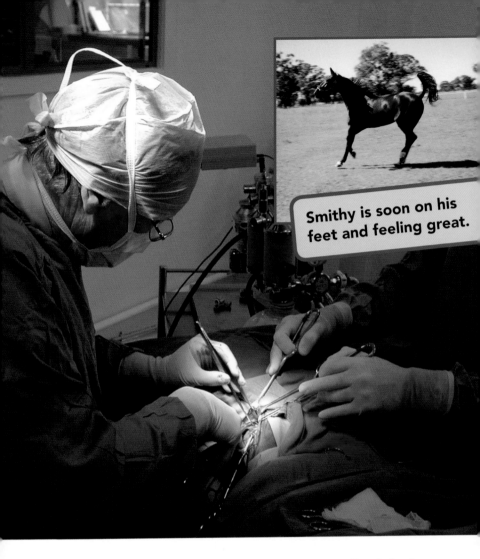

Smithy is soon on his feet and feeling great.

Vic performs the operation on Smithy's windpipe. When Vic is finished operating, Smithy will be moved to the recovery room until he wakes.

When he has recovered from the operation, he can go home with his owner.

Chapter Four

Outdoor Calls

When large animals become ill, the vet often travels to the animal. David is visiting a sick calf. He meets Liz to talk about the calf. She tells David about all of the calf's symptoms [SIMP-toms].

David must thoroughly examine the calf.
He looks in the animal's eyes and ears. He
checks inside its mouth and feels along its
body. The calf's mother watches carefully.

David checks the calf's heart rate with
the stethoscope. The calf is very sick. David
thinks it will need to be brought back to
the clinic.

A drip passes the medicine through a tube into the calf's body while it sleeps.

Back at the clinic, the calf is put into a stable. It is given medicine through an **intravenous** [in-tra-VEE-nuss] drip.

Soon it is feeling better. Once it is on its feet, the calf no longer needs the drip.

Chapter Five

X-ray

X-rays are photographs of the inside of the body.

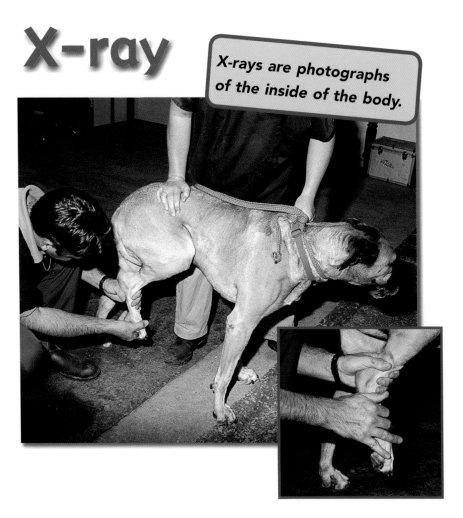

Jake the dog has a sore leg. The best way to find the problem is to x-ray the leg. An x-ray will show if Jake has any broken bones.

Jake will be given a medicine called a sedative to make him go to sleep.

First, Amanda takes Jake to the scale to be weighed. Jake must be asleep for the x-ray. The technician weighs Jake so the vet will know how much sedative to use.

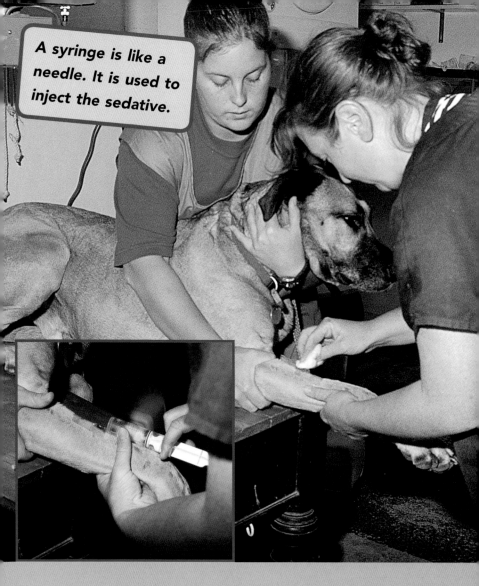

A syringe is like a needle. It is used to inject the sedative.

Jake is lifted onto the x-ray table. Amanda holds Jake still while Kellie cleans an area of Jake's leg. A syringe [sir-INGE] full of sedative is injected into Jake's leg. Soon Jake will be fast asleep.

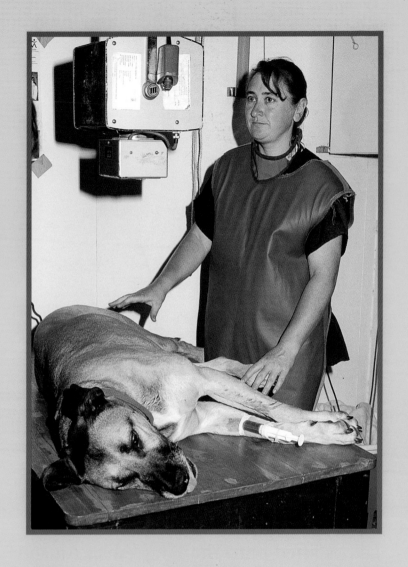

Kellie and Amanda make sure Jake is laid
out flat on the table for the x-ray. They will
x-ray one side of Jake, then turn him over
to x-ray the other side.

It's closing time at the animal clinic for another day. Jake and Buddy have been sent home. Smithy, Butch, and the calf will stay until they are better.

David has left early. He will be on call overnight in case there is an emergency. Everyone else can relax until tomorrow.

Glossary

animal clinic a place where sick and well animals are treated by vets

infection a sickness caused by germs

intravenous [in-tra-VEE-nuss] within a vein

specialist an expert

sterilizing [STARE-a-lie-zing] cleaning to prevent infection

stethoscope [STETH-a-scope] an instrument used to listen to sounds inside the body

windpipe the tube that carries air from the throat to the lungs

Index